SCI-FI OR STEM?™

HUMAN CLONING

Rosen YA
New York

KRISTI LEW

Published in 2019 by The Rosen Publishing Group, Inc.
29 East 21st Street, New York, NY 10010

First Edition

Library of Congress Cataloging-in-Publication Data

Names: Lew, Kristi, author.
Title: Human cloning / Kristi Lew.
Description: New York: Rosen Publishing, 2019. | Series: Sci-fi or STEM? | Audience: Grades 7–12. | Includes bibliographical references and index.
Identifiers: LCCN 2017047082| ISBN 9781508180340 (library bound) | ISBN 9781508180357 (pbk.)
Subjects: LCSH: Human cloning—Juvenile literature. | Human cloning—Moral and ethical aspects—Juvenile literature. | Genetic engineering—Moral and ethical aspects—Juvenile literature.
Classification: LCC QH442.2 .L49 2019 | DDC 176/.22—dc23
LC record available at https://lccn.loc.gov/2017047082

Manufactured in the United States of America

CONTENTS

INTRODUCTION

What do *Frankenstein, A Brave New World, The Hunger Games,* and *Star Wars* all have in common? They all belong to the same genre—science fiction. The science fiction, or sci-fi, genre is comprised of imaginary tales with scientific plots. Many scholars consider *Gulliver's Travels*, published in 1726, to be a precursor to the modern science fiction genre. Written by Jonathan Swift, *Gulliver's Travels* is a satirical novel that includes a flying island populated by scientists doing "useless" experiments with no practical applications.

Mary Wollstonecraft Shelley's novel *Frankenstein; or The Modern Prometheus* appeared on the scene in 1818 and today is a sci-fi classic. Long before in vitro fertilization (IVF), cloning, or keeping human cells alive in a laboratory was possible, this story challenged the wisdom and morality of creating human life by artificial means. It is often considered to be a cautionary tale of the dangers of scientific knowledge and, especially, of using that knowledge without forethought.

The science fiction genre blossomed during the late nineteenth and early twentieth centuries as new technologies were invented and scientific knowledge grew. Whether the subject is the creation

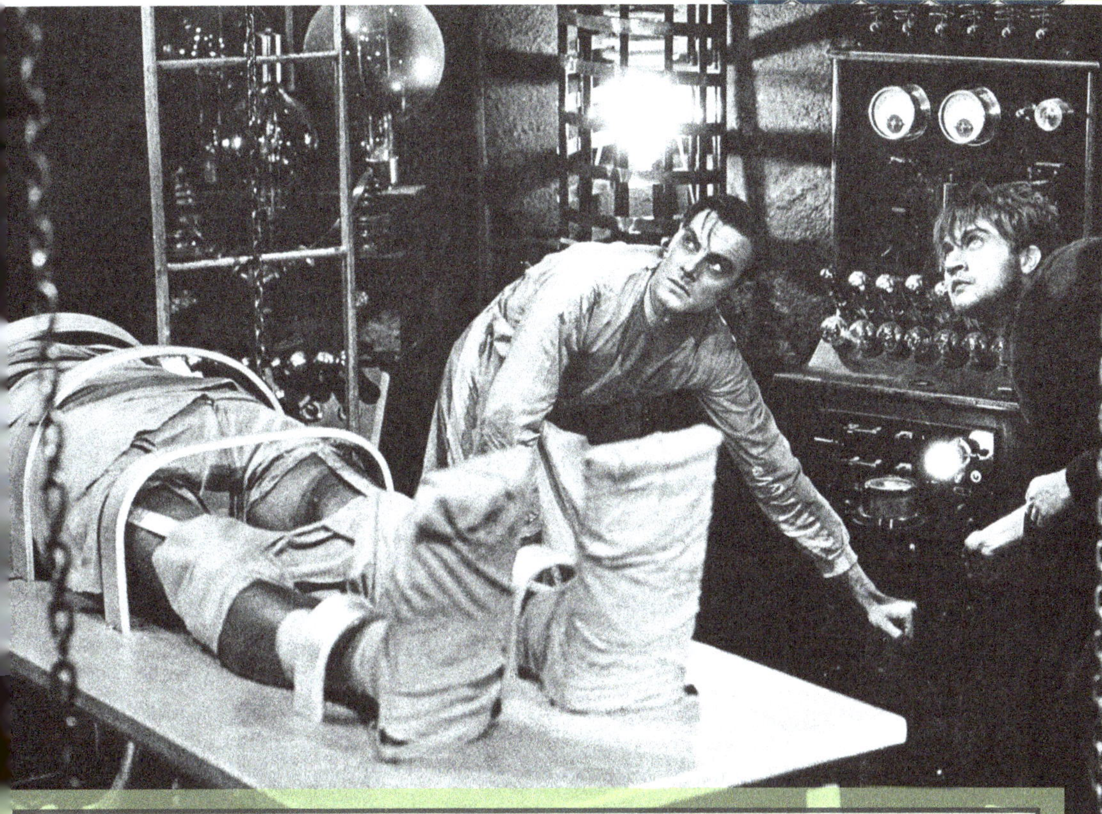

Dr. Frankenstein, played by Colin Clive, brings his monster to life in his laboratory in this scene from the 1931 film version of Mary Shelley's 1818 novel *Frankenstein; or The Modern Prometheus.*

of new life, the workings of a postapocalyptic society, space exploration, or an alien invasion, sci-fi is more popular today than it has ever been in the past.

Many people find science fiction so fascinating because these stories take technology that already exists and imagines what could happen in the future. Sci-fi authors take tiny grains of scientific truth and expand them into something that is not yet a reality. While the technology scientists and engineers are creating today serves as inspiration for sci-fi authors, the imagination of sci-fi writers often inspires scientists and engineers, too. Sometimes, it can seem as if an author's imagination has sprung to life in real time. This tie between reality and imagination is what makes science fiction so compelling.

As a genre, science fiction is exceptional in its ability to inspire curiosity about the world, how it works, and what might lie beyond it. Because sci-fi authors often draw on history and sociology, as well as science and technology, to weave their tales, reading science fiction can deepen a person's understanding of these topics, too. Sci-fi stories inspire people to examine the facts behind the fiction and to think about the future as well as how science and technology might fit into it—for better or for worse.

What if, for example, scientists could safely and reliably create human life? How would people created in a laboratory be different from people who are born of two parents? Would they be different at all? What if so-called seed ships could contain laboratories capable of conceiving, incubating, birthing, and rearing humans thousands of light-years from Earth? Some people believe this is one way the human species could be propagated throughout the universe. How might this development affect the future of human evolution? These questions and many other hypothetical scenarios bear speculation, preferably before the technology actually exists and unintended consequences become apparent. Imaginative science fiction authors and the innovative researchers currently working with cloning technologies are already pondering these issues. Anyone interested in human cloning or other tangential fields in science, technology, engineering, and mathematics (STEM) must be prepared to examine them as well.

CHAPTER 1

SCIENCE FICTION

Before delving into how human cloning is depicted in classic and modern science fiction, it is helpful to know exactly what constitutes a clone. A clone is an organism with the exact same genetic makeup as its original. In other words, a clone, whether made through artificial means or by an accident of birth, has DNA that is identical to the DNA of another being. DNA is a molecule that carries the instructions for the growth, development, functioning, and reproduction of an organism.

In sci-fi films, television series, and books, a clone may not be called a clone. Clones may be referred to by any number of made-up names, including repeaters, replicants, rebirths, relicts, duplicates, dittos, and doppelgängers. The techniques used to produce a clone vary, too. Some superheroes, like the Flash, can self-replicate when the need arises. Matter replicators are also a common trope used to create duplicates. Film creators are fond of showing clones floating in pods, tanks, jars, chambers, or some other type of containment unit.

Sci-fi authors use clones to explore certain themes. Most often, the underlying theme is: what does it mean to be human? In many works of speculative fiction, clones are either

The first successfully cloned Afghan hound (*right*) sits beside his original.

difficult to control or downright dangerous. The scientists who create them are nearly always depicted as either rogue, evil, or "mad." Alternatively, the scientists are shown as bumbling idiots who are unaware of what they are getting themselves into. Clones may be portrayed as expendable and created for military purposes, dangerous or undesirable work, or to be exploited for organ harvest. Other stories delve into the re-creation of historical figures (but only the geniuses) and bringing back of loved ones. In these stories, the expectation is always that the clones are to be carbon copies of their originals. This expectation is rarely met.

TELEVISION AND FILM

In the animated television series *Star Wars: Clone Wars,* for example, an army of clones is created by the Republic to fight against the droid army of Count Dooku. In the beginning of the series, and in the movies that follow in the timeline, the clones appear to be only expendable copies of an accomplished fighter and bounty hunter, Jango Fett. As time goes on, however, it becomes clear that, unbeknownst to the Jedi, who commissioned the army, the Sith Lords have tricked the scientists who created the clones into implanting a biochip in each clone. This chip makes the clones less aggressive than their template, Jango Fett, undermining the effectiveness of the Republic's army. Even more dangerous, it also ensures the clones' complete obedience to the directives of the Sith Lords.

The Fugitives, a 2005 dramatic British television series, does not portray clones themselves as being dangerous. Instead, it was possessing the knowledge that clones exist that put the characters in peril. The show's premise centers around a teenager named Jay Keaton. While eavesdropping one night, Jay discovers that his fa-

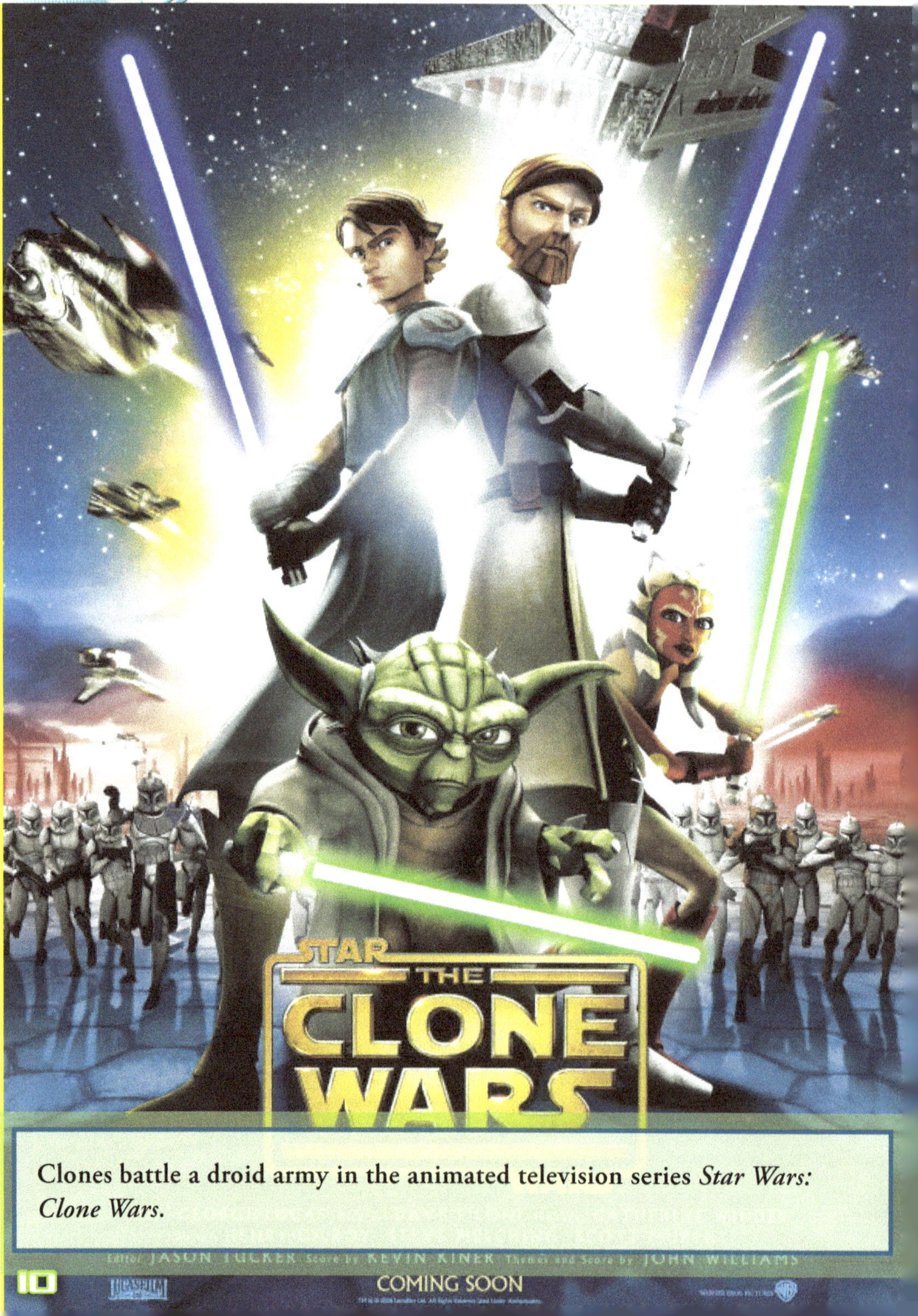

Clones battle a droid army in the animated television series *Star Wars: Clone Wars.*

ther, a brilliant scientist, once worked for EmbroGen, a genetics company that has been conducting illegal cloning experiments on children. Worried that he is about to become a test subject, Jay decides to run away from home. Before leaving, he downloads his father's computer files to a thumb drive before deleting the original files. This action puts him at odds with the cold-hearted head of the company, who orders his operatives to find and retrieve the files, no matter what the cost. While on the run, Jay meets Mel and the two of them try to figure out how to keep Jay out of the hands of the people who are bent on silencing him. Once it becomes clear to Jay that his clones are trapped in the underground laboratories of EmbroGen, the focus of his mission, and Mel's, turns to saving the clones from destruction. Unfortunately, the series lasted only one season before falling victim to budget cuts.

Another British television series, *Clone*, introduced in 2008, took a slightly lighter look at human cloning. This comedy series is the story of a brilliant scientist named Dr. Victor Blenkinsop, who, portrayed as a modern-day Dr. Frankenstein, is commissioned by the military to create the first human clone as a prototype super-soldier. To his disappointment and disgust, Blenkinsop's intended superweapon turns out to be naive and childlike. Everything is new and exciting to Clone, and he is much more likely to hug someone than kill that person. Exasperated by his creation's ignorance and innocence, but nevertheless unwilling to see him destroyed, Blenkinsop flees from his military masters and tries to find the neurological trigger he is convinced will turn Clone into the supersoldier he was intended to be.

On an even lighter note, the 2005 Canadian animated comedy series *Carl*^{2} follows the antics of fourteen-year-old Carl and the clone he accidentally orders off the internet. At first, slacker Carl is thrilled to have a clone, whom he names C2. After all, C2 can do all the things Carl does not want to do—his homework, attending school, and chores around the house. But soon, Carl realizes that C2 is not as easily controllable as he would like. A series of hilarious misadventures ensue when C2 either does exactly the opposite of what Carl wishes or takes Carl so literally that he ends up getting his original in hot water.

Several movies also depict the lighter side of cloning, including the 1996 *Multiplicity*, starring Michael Keaton and Andie MacDowell. Keaton plays the overworked Doug Kinney while McDowell portrays his increasingly confused wife. Doug Kinney wants only one thing—some time for himself, a premise that places the film firmly among those exploring the theme of being careful about what you wish for. After Doug has himself cloned, he spends the rest of the film frantically trying to rectify the mistakes his clones have made while attempting not to get caught in the same place as one of his other selves.

The Other Me is a Disney made-for-TV movie released in 2000. This comedy follows Will Browning, a young teen who accidentally clones himself while working on a science project. Will's clone turns out to be smarter, cooler, and more responsible than he is and teaches him a few truths about being human.

NOVELS

Books, and the movies that are based on them, tend to delve into deeper issues than TV series and films not based on novels. Novels are more likely to explore the behavioral adaptations—clones who do not behave, think, or feel like their originals—the emotional experiences, or the psychological ramifications of being a clone.

SCI-FI SOURCES

One of the first novels to speculate what might happen if human cloning were to become widespread is *Brave New World* by Aldous Huxley. Published in 1932, *Brave New World* never mentions the word "cloning." Instead, Huxley describes how identical people are made from a single egg using a technique called the Bokanovsky Process: "One egg, one embryo, one adult—normality. But a bokanovskified egg will bud, will proliferate, will divide. From eight to ninety-six buds, and every bud will grow into a perfectly formed embryo, and every embryo into a full-sized adult."

Though he never uses the word "clone," that is what Huxley was alluding to in his satirical depiction of a futuristic "utopian" society. In Huxley's imagined world, the Bokanovsky Process is used only for the lower classes, those who are destined for hard, mindless, physical labor. He defines the Bokanovsky Process as "progress," but is it really?

Many of the questions raised by Huxley in *Brave New World* remain unanswered. Modern novels still struggle to determine how human clones should be treated if they existed. Nancy Farmer's 2002 *The House of the Scorpion* has a particularly brutal answer: "You're a clone," [Tom] murmured. "Know what that is? A kind of puke. You were puked up by a cow."

Aldous Huxley imagined what might happen if human cloning were to become commonplace.

Books are also more likely to look at the social aspects of human cloning. For example, novels often grapple with the idea of what rights clones should have if they were to become commonplace in the future. Should clones be treated as people or as animals?

The Boys from Brazil by Ira Levin is another sci-fi classic that tackles human cloning. Published in 1976, this novel imagines what would have happened if Dr. Josef Mengele survived World War II, moved to South America, and cloned Adolf Hitler. As with other books, movies, and television series that portray the clones of famous historical figures, *The Boys from Brazi*l grapples with the concepts of identity and individuality that strike at the heart of the "nature versus nurture" debate. This long-running debate has largely been replaced by the idea that human personality and behavior are a result of both "nature," or genetics, and "nurture," the environment a child is raised within as well as his or her experiences.

More contemporary novels, such as the novel by Anthony Horowitz called *Point Blank* (in the United Kingdom, *Point Blanc* [2001]; in North America, *Point Blank* [2002]), also confront the idea of free will. *Point Blank* follows fourteen-year-old spy Alex Rider, who is assigned to an elite prep school. Alex soon finds out that all the schoolboys have been replaced by clones. The clones and the scientist who created them plot the murders of the parents of the clones' originals to abscond with their inheritances.

The House of the Scorpion (2002) and that book's sequel, *The Lord of Opium* (2013), tell the story of a boy named Matt. Matt is the clone of a powerful drug dealer named El Petrón. In author Nancy Farmer's imagined world, clone embryos are incubated and brought to term in cows and, by law, are "fixed" at birth. In this case, "fixing" means administering an injection that destroys most of the clones' brains to inhibit their IQ. This procedure is carried out because the clones are created for one purpose—as slaves for planting, tending, and harvesting opium. If they are not told to stop working, they will work themselves to death. In this world, clones are treated as animals. If they get sick, they are treated by a veterinarian, not a doctor. Children are taught to hate and fear them. They are told clones are more vicious than werewolves. Matt has escaped this fate, but not everyone is willing to treat him as human. As he grows older, Matt begins to realize that, like the other clones of the drug lord before him, he was created to provide body parts to the aging El Petrón as his original body parts

No, Anthony Horowitz, author of the popular *Alex Rider* series, has not been cloned. Instead, he uses a mirror to reproduce his image.

fail. For El Petrón, Matt is the guarantee of eternal life. For Matt, El Petrón is a death sentence.

Double Identity, a novel written by Margaret Peterson Haddix and published in 2005, moves in a slightly different direction. In this novel, Haddix explores what would happen if grieving parents were to clone a dead child. It examines the psychological ramifications of being a "duplicate" and whether or not a clone can live up to the expectations of parents expecting a carbon copy of a beloved child.

All these novels bring up questions about the ethics of human cloning. If cloning were to become commonplace, should clones be treated like everyone else? Should they be considered carbon copies of their originals? Should they be expected to be their originals' exact duplicates—act the same way and like the same things—or should they be treated as individuals? To begin to understand these issues, it may be helpful to understand exactly how cloning works, what it is—and, especially, what it is not.

CHAPTER 2

SCIENCE FACT

Humans have forty-six chromosomes. Twenty-three chromosomes come from the father and twenty-three come from the mother. When sperm and egg meet, these chromosomes mix and become a single fertilized egg, or a zygote. The zygote begins to divide—first into two cells, then into four, then eight, and so on. Once cell division begins, the embryonic period has begun.

THE CLONING PROCESS

Scientists can create clones in the laboratory in two ways—through artificial embryo splitting or by nuclear transplantation. Artificial embryo splitting, or twinning, involves dividing a very early embryo into individual cells. Once separated, these cells continue to divide and become separate embryos. Because each cell came from the same fertilized egg, they all have identical copies of the DNA molecule.

The use of nuclear transplantation to create clones is a little more involved. Nuclear transplantation is also called

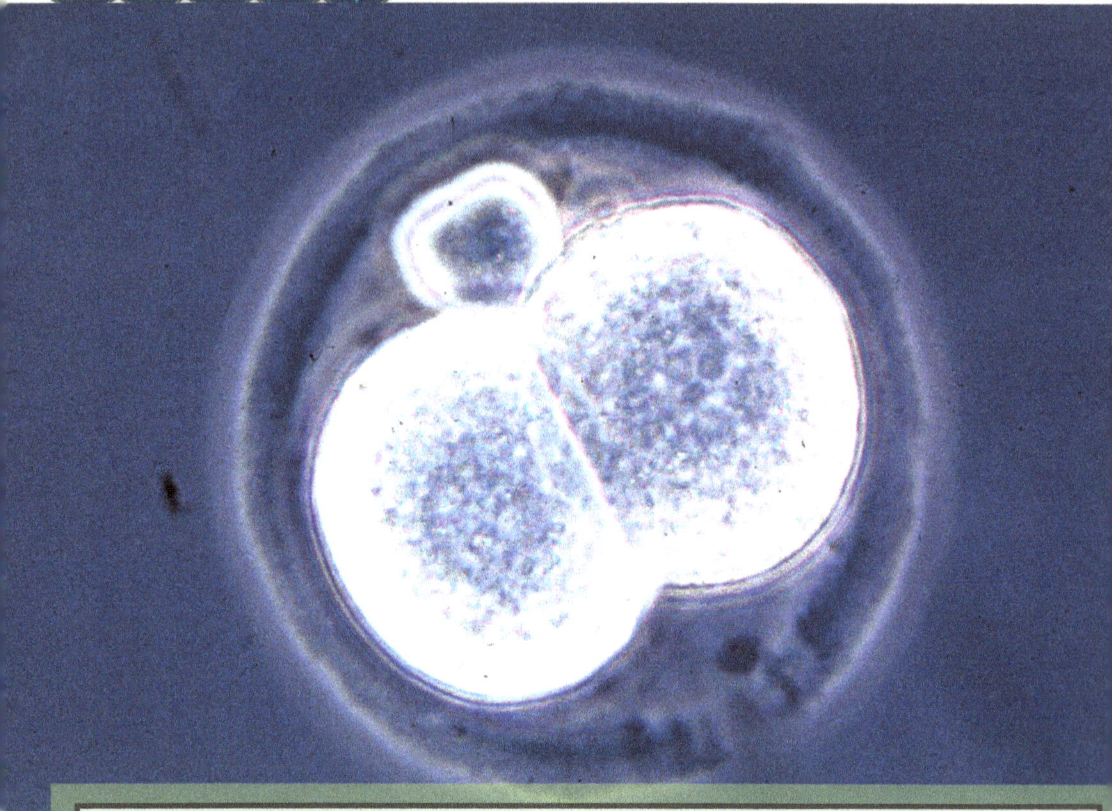

The two cells in this embryo could be artificially separated to produce genetically identical clones.

somatic cell nuclear transfer (SCNT). A somatic cell is any cell that is not a sperm or an egg. In other words, it is a body cell rather than a reproductive cell. Reproductive cells—sperm and eggs—are called germ cells. Germ cells have only twenty-three chromosomes while body cells have forty-six.

To perform SCNT, scientists remove the nucleus from an egg cell and a somatic cell. The nucleus of the somatic cell is then injected into the enucleated egg cell. An electrical current fuses the egg cell with its new nucleus and triggers the pairing into acting as a newly fertilized cell. Once the cell begins to divide, it is implanted

NATURAL CLONES

Not all clones are artificial. Clones can happen naturally, too. Many plants and single-celled organisms reproduce asexually. Asexual reproduction does not involve the fusion of a sperm and an egg. Therefore, there is no mixing of genes. Organisms that reproduce asexually have only one parent and all the offspring are clones of that parent.

Bacteria, for example, reproduce through a process called binary fission, which is the splitting of one bacterial cell into two. Many worms can reproduce through fragmentation. During fragmentation, part of the parent worm breaks off and grows into a new worm. Some plants, such as strawberries, send out runners, which are horizontal stems. Buds appear at intervals along the runners. These buds put down roots. When the runner is broken, the buds become new plants.

Most animals that reproduce asexually are invertebrates. However, there are a few, including some lizards, sharks, and snakes, that can also reproduce this way. In vertebrates, asexual reproduction is called parthenogenesis, which means "virgin birth." During parthenogenesis, female animals can give birth to young without the presence of a male. Because no sperm is involved, there is no mixing of genes and no possibility of producing males. In place of the sperm, a tiny cell, called a polar body, "fertilizes" the egg. This fusion produces the correct number of chromosomes, but all the DNA is from the mother. Some science fiction authors have expounded on this concept by creating all-female worlds in which humans reproduce through parthenogenesis.

(continued on the next page)

(continued from the previous page)

Although human parthenogenesis lies firmly in the realm of science fiction, there are natural human clones born every day. Identical twins form when a very early embryo splits, creating two separate embryos that, thereafter, develop individually. Because they come from the same fertilized egg, identical twins have identical DNA.

into a surrogate mother and carried to term. The result is an exact genetic match to the individual from which the body cell came.

A HISTORY OF ANIMAL CLONING

It may sound rather simple, but, as it turns out, some animals are much easier to clone than others. Hans Adolf Eduard Driesch created the earliest animal clone, a sea urchin, in 1891. Mammals proved to be a bit harder.

Artificial embryo twinning produced the sea urchin clone created by Driesch. Sea urchins are surprisingly easy to twin. All that is required to separate the cells in a sea urchin embryo is a nice hard shake. From his experiment, Dreisch learned that cells separated in an early stage of development could develop into two individuals. The first vertebrate created by this method was a salamander in 1902. Salamander cells weren't quite as easy to separate as those of a sea urchin. Instead of shaking, the salamander cells were separated by tying a tiny loop, made from baby hair, between the cells and pulling it until the cells separated. Hans Spemann, the

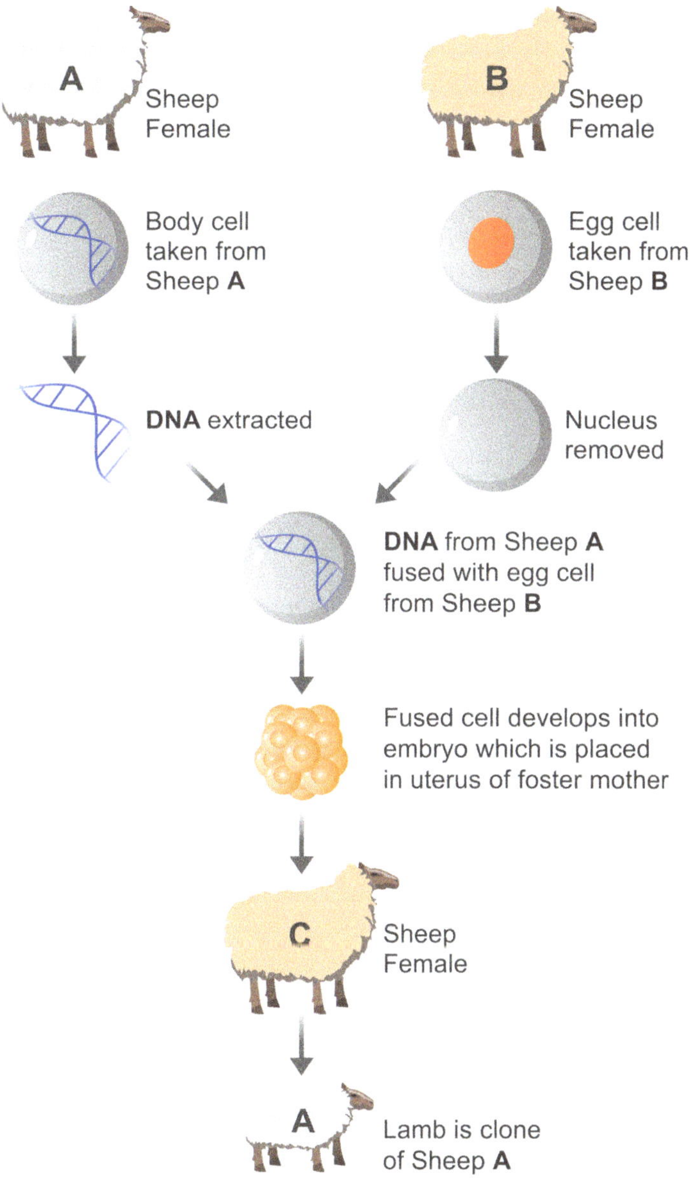

The offspring that results from somatic cell nuclear transfer (SCNT) is the clone of the animal from which the DNA came.

scientist who conducted these experiments, also tried separating salamander embryos after they had divided into more than two cells, but he was unsuccessful. What Spemann learned from these failures was that cloning a vertebrate was possible in the early stages of development but would not work after they had passed into a more advanced stage.

Robert Briggs and Thomas King carried out the first successful nuclear transfer in 1952. In this experiment, Briggs and King transferred the nucleus from an early tadpole embryo into an enucleated frog's egg. The scientists tried this experiment multiple times and found that the nucleus from an early embryo always developed into a tadpole. However, nuclei taken from a more advanced tadpole embryo either did not develop at all or did not develop normally.

John Gurdon carried out the first somatic cell nuclear transfer in 1958. Gurdon transplanted the nucleus of a tadpole intestinal cell into an enucleated frog's egg. The egg developed into a tadpole embryo and, for the first time, proved that cells from a fully developed animal could be used as cloning material.

A rabbit was the first mammal to be cloned through nuclear transfer. Mammalian eggs are much smaller than those of an amphibian, like a frog or a salamander. For this reason, Derek Bromhall, in 1975, was forced to use a glass pipette like a straw to remove the nucleus from the rabbit embryo cell and implant it into an enucleated egg. The resulting cell divided and grew into an early embryo but was never placed inside the womb of a female rabbit to see if it would continue to develop.

In 1984, Steen Willadsen removed nuclei from a sheep embryo and transplanted them into enucleated sheep cells. Using an electric shock to fuse the nucleus and the cell, Willadsen was able to get the cell to divide. He then implanted the embryos

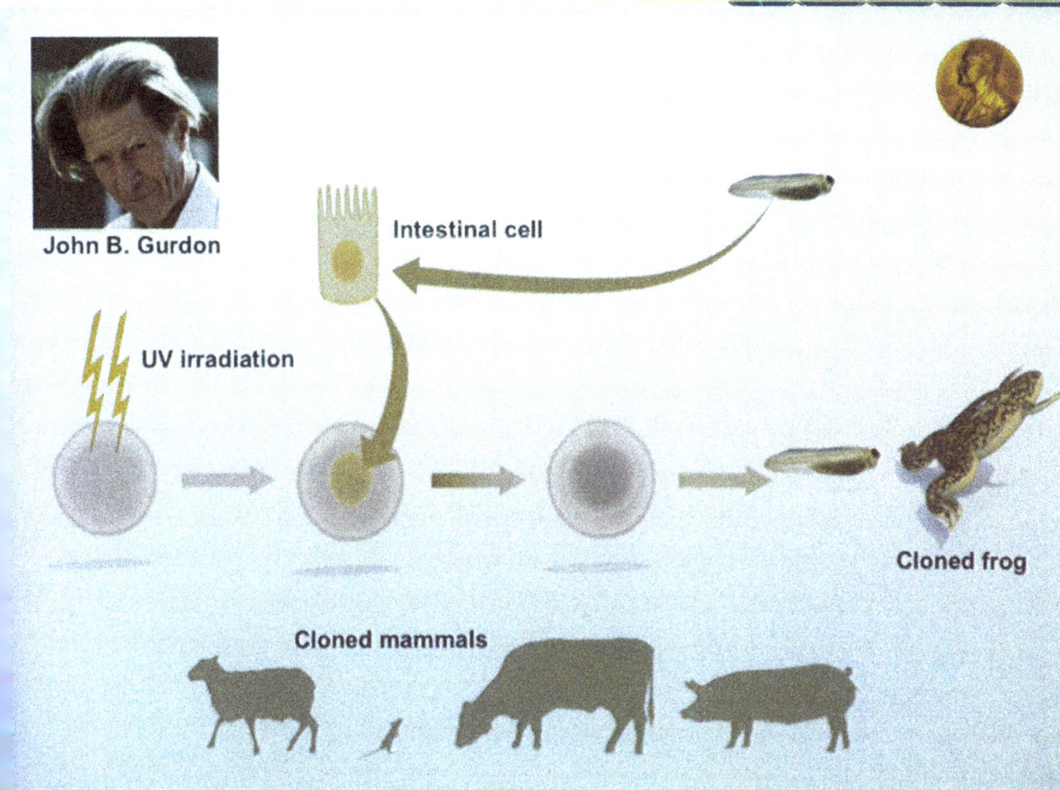

John Gurdon was awarded the 2012 Nobel Prize in Medicine for the discovery that mature body cells could be reprogrammed to divide like embryonic cells.

into a female sheep to allow them to develop further. The result was the birth of the first cloned mammals—three lambs. In 1987, the same technique was used to create two cloned calves, named Fusion and Copy. At this time, scientists did not think it was possible to clone a mammal from a somatic cell taken from an adult.

That all changed in 1996—the year that cloning first came to widespread public attention. Ian Wilmut and his colleagues at the Roslin Institute in Scotland announced the birth of a lamb named Dolly. To create Dolly, the scientists took the nucleus from the adult sheep's udder cell and placed it into an enucleated sheep cell. For the first time, scientists had proven that mammals could be cloned from adult animals.

This step was a big deal. Embryonic cells, or stem cells, can differentiate into any type of cell. However, once a cell has differentiated, the genes that are not needed for that cell's specific functions are shut down. For the nucleus of a somatic cell to act as the nucleus of an embryonic cell and start dividing, the nucleus must be "reset" to the embryonic stage. If this resetting process is not done, an embryo will not develop. It took Wilmut and his team 277 attempts to produce Dolly.

The successful birth of Dolly set off a firestorm in the media. She fascinated people. It did not require an enormous leap of imagination to envision a future in which human cloning was commonplace. This vision became even more of a reality with the cloning of the first primate, a rhesus monkey. This event occurred in 1997 through embryonic cell nuclear transfer. Multiple scientists were involved, and twenty-nine cloned embryos were created. Out of the twenty-nine, two monkeys were born, Neti and Ditto.

Between 1998 and 1999, scientists would clone more mammals, including mice, cows, and goats, through somatic cell nuclear transfer. However, it was not until 2007 that the first primate embryonic stem cells were created by SCNT. To accomplish this feat, researchers took the nucleus from an adult monkey and fused it with an enucleated monkey egg cell. The resulting embryo was allowed to develop for a short time. After about a week, the cells were removed from the embryo and placed into a petri dish with nutrients where they continued to multiply and divide. Given the right conditions, these cells can be kept alive indefinitely and they are called an embryonic stem cell line. By introducing different growth factors, embryonic stem cells can be induced to develop into any type of cell.

The scientist Ian Wilmut stands with Dolly, the first mammal cloned using DNA from an adult somatic cell.

This experiment showed that primate embryonic stem cells could be created in the laboratory and opened the door to the possibility of creating human therapeutic cloning. Therapeutic cloning is different from reproductive cloning. The goal of therapeutic cloning is to create stem cells for a specific person, cells that carry that person's DNA. The stem cells could then be used to repair or replace damaged cells, organs, or tissues.

Reproductive cloning, on the other hand, results in a new individual. In early 2018, Chinese scientists reported the birth of two long-tailed macaques successfully cloned from an adult cell. With this announcement, human reproductive cloning became more possible.

CLONES IN THE SUPERMARKET

People have been eating clones for a very long time. For example, many of the fruits people eat are clones. The most popular type of banana, called the Cavendish, creates suckers (the shoots that develop from the plants' rhizomes, or stems) to reproduce, and all these suckers are clones of an adult banana plant.

To some people, this technology makes a lot of sense. Agricultural clones could help feed the world's growing population. But others are not quite as open to this new idea. The major concern expressed by the public is whether or not animal clones are safe to eat. However, food safety is not really the issue. Clones have the same DNA as the animal they came from, which means that they are as safe to eat as the animal from which they were created. The real concern should be the loss of genetic diversity. Monoculture, or growing genetically identical crops, makes plants easier to grow (because they all have the same needs) and produces higher yields (because they are more resistant to disease). On the other hand, having the same genes also makes every plant vulnerable to the same threat, such as a newly arrived insect species or a disease. Creating clones of livestock also comes with problems, primarily the higher environmental pressures created by raising more animals.

DO HUMAN CLONES EXIST?

More than two decades have passed since Dolly the sheep was born and the world has yet to see its first human clone (other than identical twins, of course). There have been some unverified reports, but no conclusive evidence has ever been presented to show that a fully functioning human clone exists. Indeed, because of legal and ethical concerns, most research in this field is limited to therapeutic cloning, not reproductive.

In 1998, two years after Dolly was born, South Korean scientists announced that they had created a four-cell human embryo from an adult cell. However, the scientists halted the experiment at that stage, and the embryo was never implanted into a surrogate to see if it would develop further.

The same year, scientists tried to create human stem cells by fusing human skin cell nuclei with enucleated bovine (cow) eggs. The hybrid began to divide but the embryo was destroyed after twelve days. By 2009, scientists had determined that using animal eggs as surrogates for human eggs was unlikely to work because they did not "reset" to the embryonic stage correctly.

In 2001, Advanced Cell Technology (ACT) announced it had cloned a human embryo for the purposes of harvesting human stem cells and creating stem cell lines. The company used nuclear transfer to create eight fused eggs. Of the eight, two divided to form early four-celled embryos. One of the two continued to divide to the six-cell stage before it stopped.

In 2002, Clonaid, a company affiliated with the Raëlian religious movement, which believes humans were created by aliens, announced that they had created the first human clone, whom they named Eve. Yet, neither the Clonaid scientists nor the Raëlian

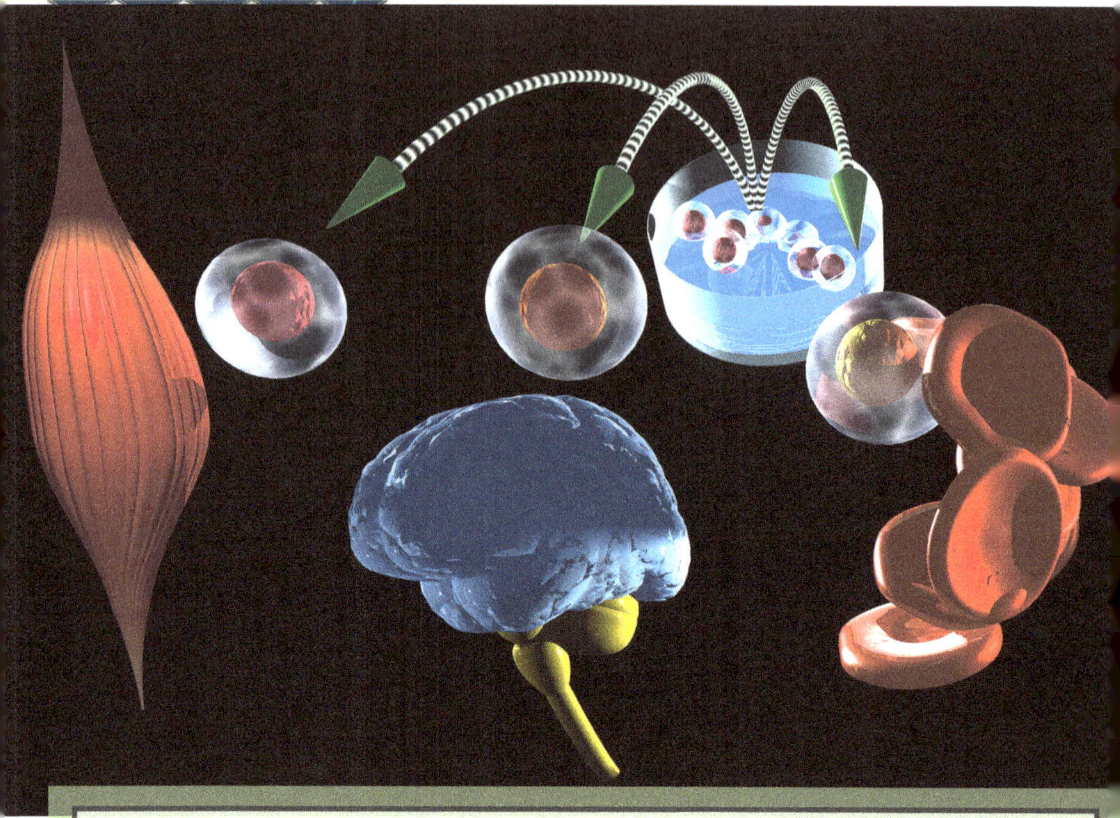

Embryonic stem cells are capable of becoming any type of body cell, including muscle cells, nerve cells, or blood cells.

leadership ever produced any concrete evidence, like photographs or a DNA test, of the child or her original. Clonaid adamantly defends their claim and say they have cloned many people. Yet they refuse to release the identities of the clones or the originals, citing privacy reasons.

In 2004, Woo-Suk Hwang of National University in South Korea published a paper in *Science* announcing the creation of the first embryonic human stem cell line produced through SCNT. However, after an independent committee found no supporting evidence of the claim, the paper was retracted in 2006.

Scientists kept trying. Finally, in 2013, Shoukhrat Mitalipov and his colleagues were successful in producing an embryonic stem cell line using SCNT. The key was finding the perfect combination of chemicals and electrical pulses that would "reprogram" the cell back to the embryonic stage. If the cells had been allowed to divide, they would have resulted in the first human clone. However, the cells were not allowed to develop beyond the embryonic stage and were instead harvested to create a stem cell line for the eight-month-old baby from which the somatic cell originated. After the false claims that had come before this breakthrough, the scientific community required substantial proof of this claim. This proof was provided and has been studied and verified to be true. In 2014, two separate research teams successfully created embryonic stem cell lines for adults, thus proving that therapeutic cloning was possible.

CHAPTER 3

SCIENCE FUTURE

Scientists have spent a great deal of time and enormous resources learning which cloning techniques work and which do not. But to what end? Why does it matter whether people can clone a sea urchin or not? Do scientists intend to make armies of cloned people? It may be easier to understand how animal cloning might assist humans in the future.

THE FUTURE OF ANIMAL CLONING

Before Dolly came along, the scientists who created her did another experiment using sheep cells that had been kept alive in a laboratory. These cells, called cultured cells, were used to produce two cloned lambs, named Megan and Morag. The birth of these lambs proved that cultured cells could be used to create viable clones. This discovery was exciting because scientists had already learned how to transfer genes into cultured cells.

The year after Dolly was born, Wilmut and his team produced Polly and Molly. Like Dolly, Polly and Molly were clones made using somatic cell nuclear transfer. Unlike Dolly, the somatic cells used to create Polly and Molly had been living in a laboratory and had been modified by the insertion of a human gene. This modification made the two sheep transgenic. A transgenic animal is one that has genes from two different species—in this case, sheep and human. The human gene that the scientists decided to transfer into the sheep DNA codes for a human blood clotting protein called factor IX. The protein, formerly obtained from human blood, is used in the treatment of hemophilia B, an X-linked recessive genetic disease caused by a

Polly (*left*), the first transgenic sheep, stands beside Dolly, the first sheep cloned using SCNT.

mutation in the factor IX gene. Polly and Molly produced factor IX protein in their milk. This experiment showed that animals could be engineered to make useful proteins that would treat human diseases, highlighting the potential medical uses of cloning.

Scientists use animal models to study human disease and treatment, too. By using clones, scientists could greatly increase the speed of drug discovery. Because of their decreased genetic variation, clones have more uniform responses to drug therapies than genetically unrelated individuals. Speeding drug discovery would help in various ways. First, it would decrease the number of animals needed for medical research studies. Second, it would get the drugs into the hands of people who desperately need them faster than the current drug discovery process. Third, it would likely save time, money, and other resources, which could potentially lower the cost of new medications.

THE FUTURE OF HUMAN CLONING

Cloning animals is one thing, but cloning a human is another issue altogether. There are quite a few problems that would need to be solved for human cloning to become a reality, much less commonplace. The first issue that would need to be addressed is the high failure rate. In species in which scientists have been successful at producing live clones, the success rate is only 1 to 4 percent, according to Ian Wilmut, as reported by the *New York Times* in 2001. That means that somewhere between 96 and 99 percent of all artificially created embryos die before birth. Remember, Dolly was the only live birth out of a total of 277 cloned embryos.

COPYCAT

In 2001, cheek cells were taken from a cat named Rainbow. Rainbow's cheek cells were used to create CC, short for carbon copy. Rainbow was a calico cat and she had a typical calico coat, meaning that she had orange patches of fur mixed with black and white patches. CC, however, had no orange fur whatsoever. Rainbow and CC were quite different in temperament, too. Rainbow had always been rather timid. CC, however, grew up to be much more curious and outgoing than her original. Even though the two cats had identical DNA, their differences showed that development is not just a matter of what genes are present. CC's coat was a different color due to an epigenetic process, in this case, one that involved the random inactivation of one of CC's X chromosomes. The differences in her behavior, on the other hand, were because of the different experiences she had while growing up.

In 2004, a California company, called Genetic Savings and Clone, Inc., announced the cloning of the first pet, a cat named Little Nicky. The woman who wanted a clone of her beloved, deceased Nicky paid $50,000 for Little Nicky. She told the Associated Press that at eight weeks old, Little Nicky was identical to her deceased pet—not only in his behavior, but also in physical signs, which included two dots inside his mouth. The scientific community was not impressed with her testimonial. Her reaction was chalked up to wishful thinking. Animal protection advocates deemed the process a ridiculous

(continued on the next page)

(continued from the previous page)

use of cloning technology, too. Their argument centered on the idea that millions of unwanted pets were put down every year. Why clone dead ones?

Copycat, or CC, was the first cloned cat. She was seven weeks old in this picture from February 14, 2002.

There are also technical issues to be solved. Primate eggs contain two proteins that are essential to cell division. These proteins are called spindle proteins. They are located very close to the chromosomes in primate eggs. When the original's DNA is removed, the spindle proteins are disrupted. This disruption interferes with cell division, which is essential to the process of cloning. Other mammals also have spindle proteins. However, in other mammals the spindle proteins are distributed throughout the nucleus and are easier to avoid when removing the DNA. Another technical issue that scientists have found is that the dyes and ultraviolet light

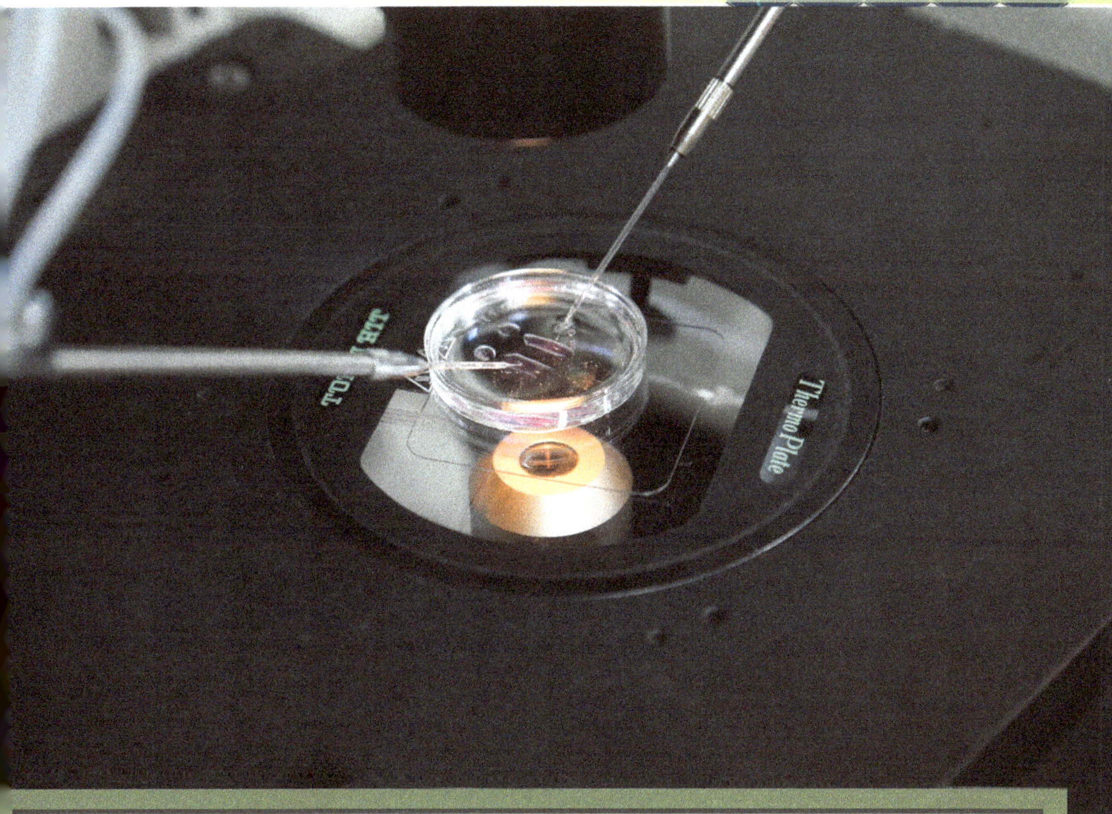

The first robotically cloned pigs were born in April 2017. Robotics, and other technologies, will probably make cloning faster, easier, and more successful in the future.

often used to remove an egg's nucleus damages primate cells and prevents them from growing normally. Some of these matters were addressed and solved with the 2018 birth of primates through somatic cell nuclear transfer, but the technique is far from being perfected.

Many people hold the view that cloned animals have poor health. Scientists have, in fact, observed some health problems in some cloned mammals. These problems include enlarged organs, impaired immune systems, premature aging, and early death. Dolly, for example, died at the age of six. The normal lifespan for sheep is twelve years. Originally, scientists thought that the reason that Dolly may have died early was because she was created using an adult cell. The common story is that Dolly was created using a cell from a six-year-old sheep and therefore she started out life with six-year-old chromosomes. This idea comes from the fact that as cells age, the tips of the chromosomes—areas called telomeres—get shorter. Eventually, the telomeres get so short that the cell will no longer divide and it dies. The theory was that because clones that originate from an adult cell begin life with shorter than normal telomeres, the clone is condemned to a shorter lifespan.

However, since Dolly's premature end, scientists have done a lot more research and have determined that this notion is not true. In fact, they have found that the cloning process "resets" telomere length. The first rigorous study of aging clones was published in 2016. It found that animal clones were just as healthy as their naturally born cohorts. Scientists from the University of Nottingham studied four clones that were created from the same batch of frozen udder cells that Dolly originated from. The clones—Debbie, Denise, Diana, and Daisy—were nine years old at the time of the study and in normal health.

The scientist who worked with Dolly reported that she died of a common respiratory infection that spread throughout the flock. Her death had nothing to do with the fact that she was a clone. When Dolly was alive, the scientists did find that she suffered from arthritis, an ailment that usually strikes older animals. However, Dolly was kept inside all her life and was often fed treats. For these reasons, many of the scientists who worked with her believe her joint problems may have been due to lifestyle rather than age.

Another popular myth is that clones cannot reproduce normally. If a clone is born and survives the first several months of

Before she died, Dolly gave birth to a lamb named Bonnie. Bonnie's birth proved that cloned animals could reproduce normally.

life, scientists have found that they will generally live out normal, healthy lives—including the ability to produce offspring by sexual reproduction, just like any other animal. The offspring of a clone are not clones. They are the same as any sexually reproduced animal.

Early attempts to clone cows resulted in some calves with health problems. Most of these issues have been resolved, however. Cloned calves are no longer any more likely to be unhealthy than those born conventionally.

Scientists have found that animal clones that are normal at birth tend to grow into strong, healthy young animals. In addition, many of the calf and lamb clones born with abnormalities may suffer from health problems in the first few months of life, but after about six months these problems tend to resolve themselves. If they survive this period, the animals are indistinguishable from conventionally bred animals of the same age.

There have been some calf and lamb fetuses that have grown too large during pregnancy. As a result, they were born with serious birth defects. These abnormalities are called large offspring syndrome, or LOS. Many people point to these problems as a concern if human cloning is to be a part of the future. However, long before cloning was even a possibility, LOS was a problem in these species from the early days of using assisted reproductive technology in livestock. Although it is true that LOS was a problem with early clones, scientists have learned more about the processes of both in vitro fertilization and cloning. As a result, the rates of LOS have decreased dramatically in cows and sheep. The syndrome has never been seen in pig or goat clones.

Although scientists no longer believe that clones are inherently unhealthier than their conventional counterparts, the myth persists, especially on the internet. Websites spreading this misinformation include the National Institutes of Health's National Human Genome Research Institute's fact sheets (for example, the one on cloning that was reviewed in March 2017). The Food and Drug Administration (FDA) website, however, updated in 2015, includes the corrected information.

Cloning technology has come a long way since the creation of Dolly. Regardless, most scientists believe cloning humans remains unfeasible, that the level of risk is unacceptable, and that there is no scientific benefit to the procedure that would outweigh its risks. The barriers to human cloning are less of a technological issue and more of an ethical one. Before human cloning could become a reality, much less commonplace, those ethical issues would need to be resolved.

CHAPTER 4

HUMAN CLONING: YES OR NO?

What exactly are the ethical considerations of human cloning? Ethics is a branch of philosophy that deals with the concepts of right and wrong. It seeks to resolve questions of what conduct is moral and what is not.

In what circumstances might human cloning be ethical? Here, many scientists draw a line between therapeutic cloning and reproductive cloning. Remember that therapeutic cloning is the cloning of cells to create a cell line that is patient specific. The hope is that these cell lines could be used to replace tissues and cells that have been damaged by an accident or disease. For example, it may be possible to replace pancreatic cells in patients with type 1 diabetes with cells that produce insulin normally. Another example is the possibility of replacing nerve cells in patients with severed spinal cords, restoring mobility to paralyzed body parts. For this use, many scientists see cloning as beneficial to humanity. Reproductive cloning, however, becomes more fraught with problematic scenarios.

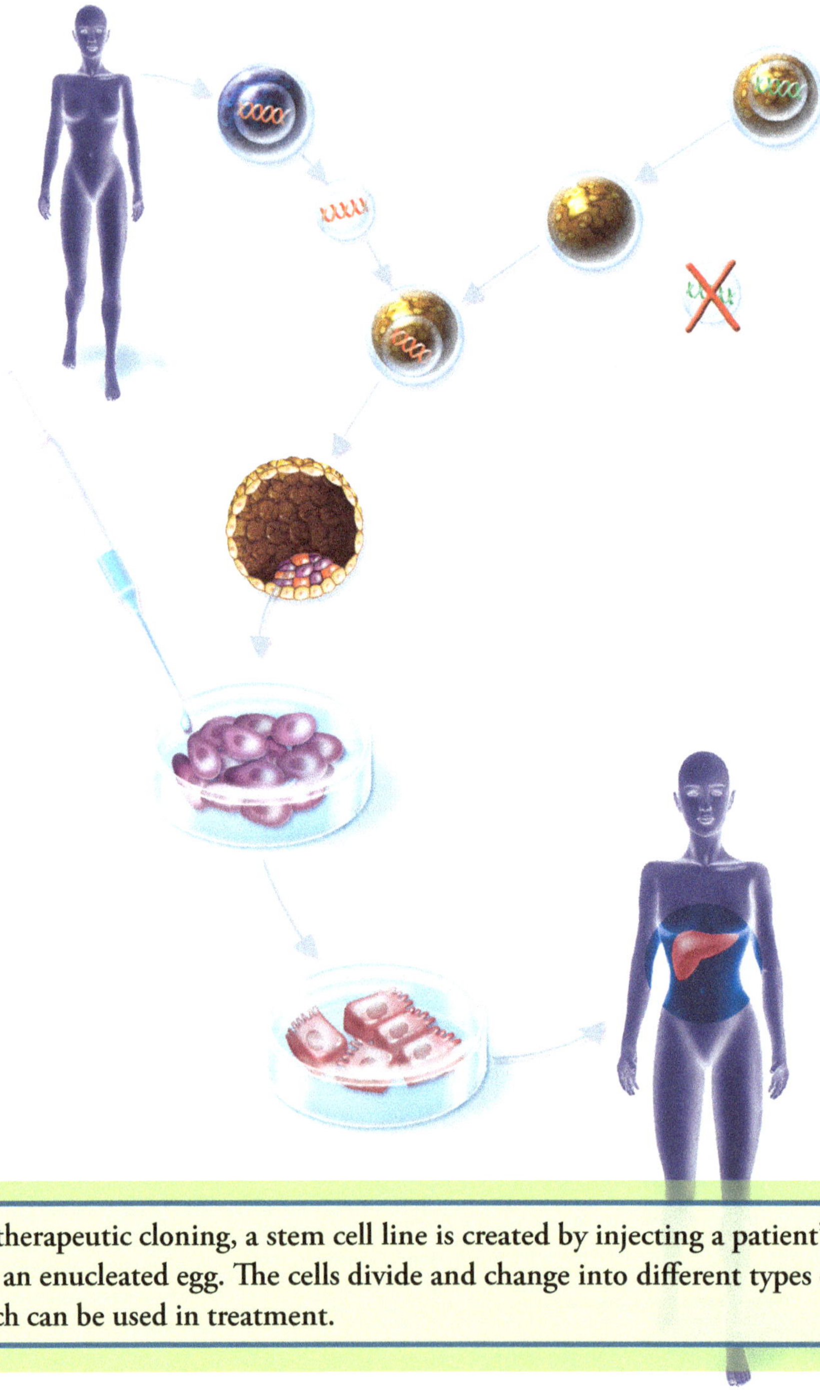

For therapeutic cloning, a stem cell line is created by injecting a patient's DNA into an enucleated egg. The cells divide and change into different types of cells, which can be used in treatment.

REASONS TO CONSIDER HUMAN REPRODUCTIVE CLONING

What are some of the reasons human reproductive cloning might be considered desirable? One reason might be to help a couple who cannot have a child naturally. Cloning might be a way to allow infertile couples to have a baby who is genetically related to one of his or her parents. One argument against this idea of producing more children is the number of children who are already looking for adoptive parents. The only reason cloning might be more desirable than adoption is that the child's medical history might be more complete if the child were cloned. As cloned animals have proved, however, the health, behavior, and physical features of a clone do not necessarily mimic that of the parent.

Another argument is what happens to the baby if the parents divorce? Does the clone automatically live with its mother (many US states award custody to the mother), its father, or its original? What happens if the baby looks like a noncustodial parent? Will there be forthcoming problems if the parent who has custody of the baby takes out his or her resentment or anger toward the noncustodial parent on the baby? (Keep in mind that the cloned human would resemble its original more than a child who is conceived by sexual reproduction because it has 100 percent of the original's genes, not 50 percent.)

Another reason people might consider cloning is to eliminate the risk of passing on a hereditary disease. However, many hereditary diseases can be detected during in vitro fertilization through preimplantation screening. During this process, scientists test fertilized eggs to determine whether or not the zygote contains the genetic misprint. If it does, that embryo is not implanted in the mother. It is destroyed. If techniques already exist to avoid this situation, why resort to cloning?

Some proponents of human cloning cite the ability to provide an exact genetic match for purposes of organ donation as a vote

If both parents carry a mutated gene (green) that causes a recessive genetic disease, there is a 25 percent chance with each pregnancy that that child will inherit the disease. There is a 50 percent chance that their offspring will carry the mutated gene and possibly pass it on to the next generation.

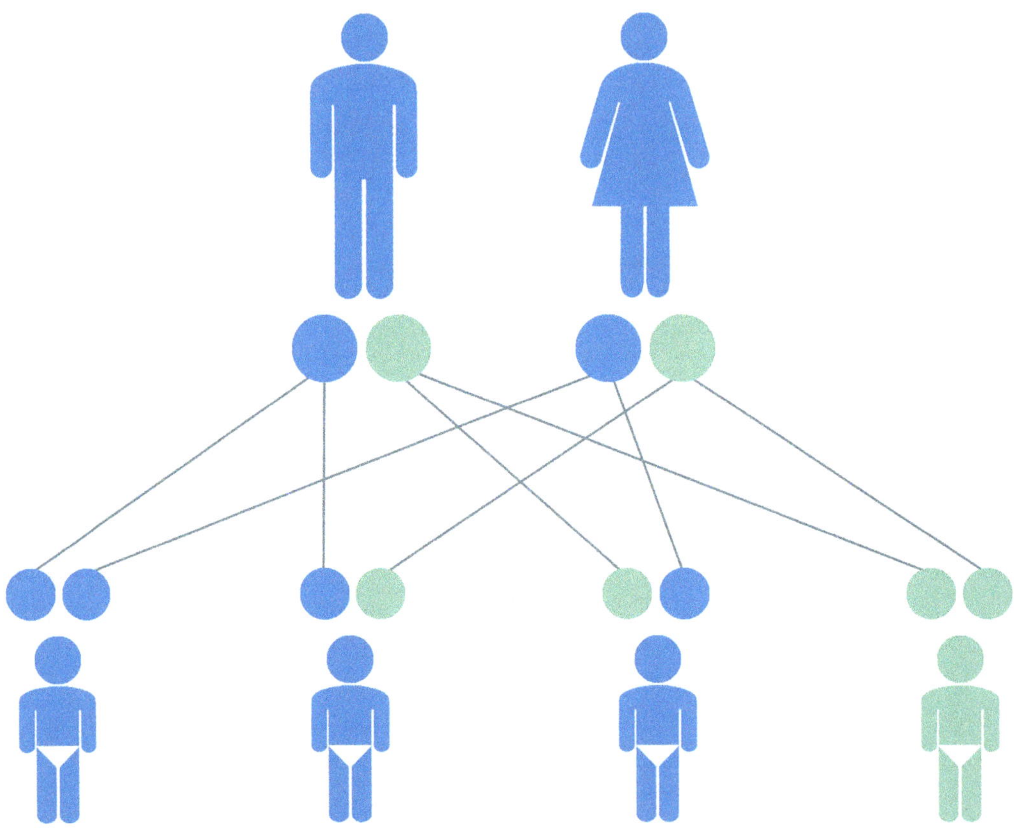

in favor of the procedure. Certainly, this might be appropriate for therapeutic cloning—where tissues are created from cells—but is it appropriate to create children for the purposes of harvesting their organs? It is a popular theme in science fiction, but most people do not think it is a proper procedure in the real world.

Surprisingly, this scenario has already played out in real life, albeit in a limited way. Sometimes called savior siblings, babies have been conceived through in vitro fertilization in the hopes that the child will eventually provide an organ or cell transplant to a fatally ill brother, sister, or parent. Preimplantation genetic analysis allows parents and doctors to determine if an embryo is a match for the ailing sibling or parent before the pregancy is carried to term. For the most part, savior siblings have been limited to solutions for blood-related genetic diseases and their donations to their siblings are generally limited to bone marrow stem cells. Bone marrow stem cells differentiate into all the other types of blood cells. The novel *My Sister's Keeper* (2004) by Jodi Picoult explores the psychological ramifications of being a savior sibling.

Double Identity (2005) by Margaret Peterson Haddix looks into another reason people might be in favor of human reproductive cloning—the possibility of cloning a dead or dying child. Written from the clone's perspective, this novel delves into the emotional and psychological complications of finding out one has been deliberately created to mimic someone else. Beyond the consequences of such an action to the clone, arguments against cloning deceased children and other relatives go back to the question of the current size of the human population and, specifically, children who already exist without a family to call their own.

CARBON COPY

In *Double Identity* by Margaret Peterson Haddix, parents find a way to clone their dead daughter, Elizabeth, who died in a car crash on her thirteenth birthday. The clone, Bethany, is approaching her thirteenth birthday when her parents start acting strange. Late one night, her parents furtively pack her up, drive to a strange town, and leave her with family members she never knew existed. When she finds videotapes of Elizabeth, Bethany suddenly realizes why everyone in town looks as if they have seen a ghost when they encounter her.

In the novel, Bethany is portrayed as looking and acting nearly identical to her original. However, as CC, Rainbow the cat's clone, proved, there is more to a clone than a carbon copy. Outside influences can help determine, or at least influence, both physical characteristics and behavior. After all, even identical human twins don't always look exactly the same, and they often act very differently, even though they have the same genetic material.

Although Haddix describes Bethany as being born an infant and growing into a teenager in *Double Identity*, some sci-fi novels, films, and television shows like to perpetrate cloning myths. Particularly, the one in which clones are "born" the same age as their originals. Both the television show *Carl*^{2} and the movie *Multiplicity* use this device to great comic effect. But, of course, in reality this is not the case. Animal clones, like Dolly, are born as babies, just like any other newborn animal. If human clones were ever created, they would be born as babies, too.

ARGUMENTS AGAINST HUMAN REPRODUCTIVE CLONING

Science fiction does a great job at exploring, and exploiting, the fears people often have toward new scientific knowledge or technology. Many arguments against human cloning, including therapeutic cloning, are based on myths, outdated information or misinformation, or the dramatic scenarios that, although fun to read, write, and think about, are not necessarily based on any reality.

Some of the concerns that fall into this category include the safety of cloning and possibility of creating armies of robotlike humans who all speak, think, and act exactly alike. The idea that cloning is not safe and that clones are unhealthy has been disproved with scientific studies, but the myth of grotesque birth defects in clones persists. There is, however, a very real ethical dilemma when it comes to the success rate of bringing cloned embryos to term. Is one living clone worth hundreds of failed attempts? For people who believe that a fertilized egg is the beginning of human life, the answer is usually no. Even people who believe life begins at a later stage struggle with the moral implications of this part of the process, though. This debate of when exactly human life begins is ongoing and has repercussions for both therapeutic and reproductive cloning.

Beyond the technicalities of whether or not human cloning is possible lie the more interesting questions of its morality. Is it right and what might be the unintended consequences of using

There are more than seven billion people on Earth, and not everyone has access to the resources they need. Is it ethical to create more people through human cloning?

this technology? For example, the world's population is well over seven billion and it continues to grow. The human population is already outstripping the available natural resources on Earth. What advantage could there be to making more people through cloning?

And in a related issue, what rights would a clone have to those natural resources? Should clones be treated the same way natural-born humans are treated? Would natural-born humans discriminate against them? In *The House of the Scorpion*, author Nancy Farmer explores the plight of clones who are created to serve as slaves. In Aldous Huxley's *Brave New World*, the upper-class Alphas and Betas are not cloned. Only lower classes are cloned, and the clones do all the manual labor in that world. If human cloning were to become commonplace, what safeguards need to be put into place so that existing class problems are not exacerbated?

Speaking of class problems, cloning would probably be expensive, at least initially. What happens if only the wealthy can afford to clone themselves? A science fiction trope related to this idea is using cloning to duplicate people with great intellect, talent, character, or other desirable traits. Often, this involves the re-creation of great scientists, musicians, artists, or politicians—not all of whom, like Hitler in *The Boys of Brazil*, should be brought back to life. But who decides who gets to be cloned? Some cultures prize one sex or one race over others. What if only people of one sex or that specific race were cloned? How might this choice affect society?

Other popular science fiction themes include creating clones with the intention of using them for their organs or solely to fight wars. Organ or tissue donation may be ethical if it is limited to living tissue, such as blood, bone marrow, or skin grafts, or to organs that can be harvested without killing the clone, such as a kidney. However, where should the line be drawn? Under what moral principles would creating people with the intention of killing them be allowed and how would this affect the clones and their creators psychologically?

A more realistic problem that could occur if human cloning were to become commonplace is a loss of genetic diversity. There is a biological advantage to sexual reproduction. The mixing of genes to create a new generation offers safeguards against disease and reduces vulnerability to other environmental factors, such as climate change. How might this loss of biodiversity affect the future of humankind?

When Dolly the sheep was first produced, newspapers and magazines were filled with fantastical imaginings. They predicted that, someday, people would clone themselves to have a complete set of spare organs. They would be continually updated with brand-

If humans were ever to be artificially cloned, it is unlikely they would be carbon copies of their originals. Instead, they would be more like their natural counterparts—identical twins.

new parts. If children were tragically lost, they could be replaced. People could make copies of themselves so they could be more productive at work and at home and somewhere, someone, would bring monsters like Adolf Hitler back from the dead.

But human cloning probably would look nothing like the way it is portrayed in books, films, and in the media. Instead, human clones would more closely resemble identical twins. They might have some things in common with their originals, but they would not be carbon copies. In fact, clones and their originals would probably have even less in common than identical twins because they would not share the same womb nor would they share the same upbringing. Years or generations would likely separate them from their originals, which means they would have a completely different set of experiences.

Scientists do not believe there are any technical problems that could not be overcome to clone humans. However, they do believe many ethical and societal issues need to be worked out before the technology is used. Science fiction authors and Hollywood will continue to fan the flames of doubt and uncertainty. As a result, many people remain fearful of the idea of human cloning. Rather than fearing what might be, thoughtful consumers of sci-fi should begin to think about how human cloning could change the human condition—for better and for worse. Only by thinking these matters through before they occur can people make rational choices based on reality. What can be imagined can come true and, sometimes, the realization of a dream is closer than it seems.

TIMELINE

1891 The first animal clone, a sea urchin, is created by Hans Adolf Eduard Driesch.

1902 The first vertebrate clone, a salamander, is created.

1932 *Brave New World* by Aldous Huxley is published.

1952 Scientists carry out the first successful nuclear transfer on an amphibian cell.

1958 The first successful somatic cell nuclear transfer is carried out on an amphibian cell.

1975 The first mammal, a rabbit, is cloned through nuclear transfer.

1978 The first child conceived through in vitro fertilization is born.

1984 The first cloned mammals are born through embryonic nuclear transfer.

1996 Dolly the sheep is cloned from an adult cell.

1997 The first primates are cloned through embryonic nuclear transfer.

2000 Geron Corporation receives a British patent covering cloning techniques and early-stage human embryo clones.

2001 The first human embryo is cloned for therapeutic stem cell research.

2002 Clonaid announces the birth of the first human clone. The scientific community believes it to be a hoax.

2004 South Korean scientists announce the creation of the first human embryonic stem cell line created through SCNT. The paper is retracted two years later after the claim fails to stand up to scrutiny.

2007 The first primate embryonic stem cell line is created through SCNT.

2013 The first verified human embryonic stem cell line is produced through SCNT.

2014 The first human embryonic stem cell line using somatic cells from an adult is created through SCNT.

2018 Chinese scientists announce the birth of the first primates cloned from an adult cell.

GLOSSARY

asexual reproduction Reproduction that does not involve the fusion of reproductive cells.

chromosome A structure, made up of DNA and proteins, which is passed from parent to offspring.

cultured cells Cells that are grown, fed, and cared for in a laboratory.

deoxyribonucleic acid (DNA) A molecule that carries the instructions for growing, developing, and maintaining an organism.

embryo A zygote that has started to divide.

enucleate To take the nucleus out of a cell.

epigenetic Referring to a process by which genetic information is changed without changing the DNA molecule.

ethics A branch of philosophy that deals with moral principles.

gene Sections of DNA that carry instructions for how to make specific proteins.

genome An organism's complete set of genes.

genre A category of art that has similarities in subject matter, style, or form.

germ cell A reproductive cell that has half the number of chromosomes as a body cell.

in vitro fertilization (IVF) A process in which an egg cell is fertilized outside a female's body, and the resulting embryo is implanted to be brought to term.

nucleus An organelle which carries most of the genetic material; also called the command center of a cell.

parthenogenesis The development of an egg without fertilization.

postapocalyptic A story that takes place after a catastrophic event, such as a nuclear war.

recessive An inherited condition in which two copies of a mutation must be present for the characteristic to be expressed.

reproductive cloning The creation of a new individual through cloning techniques.

satire The use of humor, exaggeration, or irony to spotlight ridiculous ideas or actions.

science fiction (sci-fi) Fictional stories with imagined scientific plots.

sexual reproduction Reproduction that involves the fusion of reproductive cells and the mixing of genes.

somatic cell A body cell with a full chromosome complement.

somatic cell nuclear transfer (SCNT) The process in which the nucleus of a somatic cell is transferred to an enucleated egg cell.

STEM An acronym that stands for science, technology, engineering, and mathematics.

stem cell An undifferentiated cell that is capable of transforming into any type of cell in the body.

surrogate Someone who takes over the role or job of someone else; a substitute.

telomere A section at the end of a DNA molecule.

therapeutic cloning The creation of cloned human cells and tissues with the intent that they will provide treatment for damaged or destroyed tissues or organs.

transgenic Relating to organisms that contain the genes of more than one species.

trope A storytelling shortcut that describes situations a storyteller can reasonably assume the audience will have encountered before and will recognize.

X-linked Characteristics or conditions controlled by genes that lie on the X chromosome.

zygote A fertilized egg.

Canadian Bioethics Society
740 Avenue Docteur Penfield, Suite 5200
Montreal, QC H3A-OG1
Canada
(514) 887-7030
Website: https://www.bioethics.ca
Email: info@bioethics.ca
Facebook: @canadianbioethicssociety
A nonprofit organization, the Canadian Bioethics Society serves as a forum to anyone interested in discussing, advancing, and learning more about the field of bioethics.

Canadian Coalition for Genetic Fairness (CCGF)
151 Frederick Street, Suite 400
Kitchener, ON N2H 2M2
Canada
(800) 998-7398
Website: http://ccgf-cceg.ca
Email: info@ccgf-cceg.ca
Twitter: @GeneticFairness
The CCGF is an organization that is concerned with preventing discrimination against individuals based on their genetic makeup.

Center for Genetics and Society
1122 University Avenue, #100
Berkeley, CA 94702
(510) 665-7760
Website: https://www.geneticsandsociety.org
Email: info@geneticsandsociety.org
Facebook: @GeneticsandSociety
Twitter: @C_G_S
YouTube: @geneticsandsociety
The Center for Genetics and Society is a nonprofit organization that encourages the responsible use of genetic information and reproductive technologies.

Council for Responsible Genetics
5 Upland Road, Suite 3
Cambridge, MA 02140
(617) 868-0870
Website: http://www.councilforresponsiblegenetics.org
Email: crg@gne-watch.org
A nonprofit organization, the Council for Responsible Genetics provides information and fosters debate about the societal, ethical, and environmental issues

surrounding genetic technologies.

National Human Genome Research Institute (NHGRI)
9000 Rockville Pike
Bethesda, MD 20892-2152
(301) 402-0911
Website: https://www.genome.gov
Facebook: @genome.gov
Twitter: @genome_gov
YouTube: @genometv
Created in 1989 to map the human genome, the NHGRI now studies and provides educational opportunities for scientists and students in the areas of specific genetic diseases and the genetic components of complex human illnesses.

The Roslin Institute
The University of Edinburgh
Easter Bush
Midlothian EH25 9RG
United Kingdom
+44 (0)131 651 7320
Website: https://www.ed.ac.uk/roslin
Facebook: @theroslininstitute
Twitter: @roslininstitute
The goal of the Roslin Institute is to improve the lives of animals and humans through research in animal biology and the biosciences. In 1996, scientists at Roslin cloned the first mammal, Dolly the Sheep, from an adult cell.

United States Food and Drug Administration (FDA)
10903 New Hampshire Avenue
Silver Spring, MD 20993
(888) 463-6332
Website: https://www.fda.gov
Facebook: @FDA
Twitter: @US_FDA
YouTube: @USFoodandDrugAdmin
The FDA is a governmental agency that is responsible for making sure that drugs and medical devices are not harmful to use and that the nation's food supply is safe for human consumption.

FOR FURTHER READING

Barber, Nicola. *Cloning and Genetic Engineering*. New York, NY: Rosen Publishing, 2013.

Castle, M. E. *Popular Clone*. New York, NY: Egmont USA, 2013.

Claybourne, Anna, and Stephen Moncrieff. *The Usborne Introduction to Genes & DNA*. Tulsa, OK: EDC Publishing, 2016.

Farmer, Nancy. *The House of the Scorpion*. New York, NY: Atheneum Books for Young Readers, 2013.

Farmer, Nancy. *The Lord of Opium*. New York, NY: Atheneum Books for Young Readers, 2013.

Frade, B. A., and Stephanie True Peters. *Clone Camp*. Boston, MA: Little, Brown and Company, 2017.

Gerdes, Louise I. *Human Genetics*. Farmington Hills, MI: Greenhaven Press, 2014.

Henneberg, Susan. *Cloning*. Costa Mesa, CA: Saddleback Educational Publishing, 2015.

Henneberg, Susan. *Genetic Engineering*. New York, NY: Greenhaven Publishing, 2017.

Horowitz, Anthony. *Point Blank*. New York, NY: Speak, 2008.

Rogers, Kara, ed. *Cloning*. New York, NY: Britannica Educational Publishing, 2016.

Wolfe, James, ed. *Genetic Testing and Gene Therapy*. New York, NY: Britannica Educational Publishing, 2016.

Wood, Matthew Brenden. *The Science of Science Fiction*. White River Junction, VT: Nomad Press, 2017.

BIBLIOGRAPHY

Edwards, Caroline. "Writing the Future: A Timeline of Science Fiction Literature." BBC. Retrieved August 12, 2017. http://www.bbc.co.uk/timelines/zp7dwmn.

Goldenberg, Suzanne, and Alok Jha. "The World's First Cloned Pet (Cost $50,000)." *The Guardian*, December 24, 2004. https://www.theguardian.com/world/2004/dec/24/sciencenews.genetics.

Heine, Steven J. *DNA Is Not Destiny: The Remarkable, Completely Misunderstood Relationship Between You and Your Genes.* New York, NY: W. W. Norton & Company, Inc., 2017.

Katz, Brigit. "Scientists Successfully Clone Monkeys, Breaking New Ground in a Controversial Field." Smithsonian.com. January 25, 2018. https://www.smithsonianmag.com/smart-news/two-cloned-monkeys-scientists-break-new-ground-controversial-field-180967950/.

Kolata, Gina. "In Cloning, Failure Far Exceeds Success." *New York Times*, December 11, 2001. http://www.nytimes.com/2001/12/11/science/in-cloning-failure-far-exceeds-success.html?mcubz=3.

Maienschein, Jane. *Whose View of Life? Embryos, Cloning, and Stem Cells*. Cambridge, MA: Harvard University Press, 2003.

National Human Genome Research Institute. "Cloning." March 21, 2017. https://www.genome.gov/25020028/cloning-fact-sheet.

Schaetzlein, Sonja, Andrea Lucas-Hahn, Erika Lemme, Wilfried A. Kues, Martina Dorsch, Michael P. Manns, Heiner Niemann, and K. Lenhard Rudolph. "Telomere Length Is Reset During Early Mammalian Embryogenesis." Proceedings of the National Academy of Sciences (PNAS), May 25, 2004. http://www.pnas.org/content/101/21/8034.full?tab=author-info.

Stein, Rob, and Michaeleen Doucleff. "Scientists Clone Human Embryos to Make Stem Cells." National Public Radio, May 15, 2013. http://www.npr.org/sections/health-shots/2013/05/15/183916891/scientists-clone-human-embryos-to-make-stem-cells.

United States Food and Drug Administration. "Animal Cloning." Retrieved August 13, 2017. https://www.fda.gov/animalveterinary/safetyhealth/AnimalCloning/default.htm.

University of Utah Genetic Science Learning Center. "Cloning." Retrieved August 12, 2017. http://learn.genetics.utah.edu/content/cloning.

Weintraub, Karen. "Send in the Clones: Cloned Mammals Are Just as Healthy as Their "Natural" Counterparts." *Scientific American*, October 1, 2016. https://www.scientificamerican.com/article/send-in-the-clones-cloned-mammals-are-just-as-healthy-as-their-natural-counterparts.

Wilmut, Ian. "Cloning." New Scientist. Instant Expert 2. Retrieved September 26, 2017. https://www.newscientist.com/data/doc/teaser/mm/201010/instant_expert_2_-_cloning.pdf.

Wilmut, Ian, Keith Campbell, and Colin Tudge. *The Second Creation: Dolly and the Age of Biological Control.* New York, NY: Farrar, Straus and Giroux, 2000.

Wilmut, Ian, and Roger Highfield. *After Dolly: The Uses and Misuses of Human Cloning.* New York, NY: W. W. Norton & Company, 2006.

INDEX

ABOUT THE AUTHOR

Kristi Lew is the author of numerous books for teachers and young readers. Fascinated with science from a young age, she studied biochemistry and genetics in college. Before beginning her writing career, she worked in genetics laboratories and taught high-school science. When she's not writing, she enjoys reading, traveling, sailing, and kayaking. She lives with her husband and their three fabulous felines in St. Petersburg, Florida.

PHOTO CREDITS

Cover, p. 1 Laguna Design/Science Photo Library/Getty Images; pp. 4, 7, 17, 30, 41 NikoNomad/Shutterstock.com; p. 5 Bettmann /Getty Images; pp. 8, 18 Handout/Getty Images; p. 10 RGR Collection/Alamy Stock Photo; p. 13 Charles Sheeler/Conde Nast Collection/Getty Images; p. 15 Paul Hackett/Corbis News/Getty Images; p. 21 Artwork studio BKK/Shutterstock.com; p. 23 Jonathan Nackstrand/AFP/Getty Images; p. 25 Colin McPherson/Corbis Historical/Getty Images; p. 28 Jean-Paul Joubert/Science Source; pp. 31, 37 © AP Images; p. 34 FEMA/Getty Images; p. 35 Visual China Group/ Getty Images; pp. 38–39 The Sydney Morning Herald/Fairfax Media/Getty Images; p. 42 BSIP/Universal Images Group/Getty Images; p. 44 Mikkel Juul Jensen/Science Source; pp. 48–49 Mitchell Funk/Photographer's Choice/Getty Images; p. 51 Blend Images/ Shutterstock.com; back cover and interior pages (circular element), interior pages (grid and circuit board patterns) Titima Ongkantong/ Shutterstock.com.

Design: Nelson Sá; Layout: Tahara Anderson; Senior Editor: Kathy Kuhtz Campbell; Photo Researcher: Nicole Baker